WHAT'S NEXT
NOW THAT I'M SAVED!

CHARLES J. BENNETT III

What's Next Now That I'm Saved?

Editorial assistance by Caryn Newman
Cover by Charles J. Bennett III

ISBN: 978-0-9907195-2-6

All scriptures are taken from the King James Version and the New International Version unless otherwise noted.

For further information about this title or permission, contact TLB Bookkeeping Services @ publishing@tlbbookkeeping.com.

Table of Content

Welcome To The Family

LET ME BE THE FIRST TO SAY WELCOME Home! Welcome to the family of God! In case you didn't know, there is a celebration going on in heaven at this very moment!

Luke 15:10 NKJV "Likewise, I say to you, there is joy in the presence of the angels of God over one sinner who repents."

The decision you just made to accept Jesus Christ as your Lord and Savior is by far the greatest, and most important decision you will ever make in your entire life. The reason is, this decision has both natural and spiritual implications. This decision secures your today as well as your tomorrow. It redefines your identity, restores your relationship with God, and realigns your destiny with His divine purpose for your life. Now I know there are a lot of questions that may be going through your mind right now, and that is why we are here, and it is the reason for this mini book.

Why is this information important? Well, in the natural sense, a child's formative years, or the first few years of a child's life, are critical. Something tremendous happens during the first years of our lives. Our basic learning skills, as well as, mental and physical development begin to occur. These building blocks influence the rest of our lives. Patterns are formed, habits are established, and understanding begins to take shape in ways that often determine long-term growth and stability.

The same is true for the decision you just made for Christ. The decisions you make and the steps you take starting TODAY will have a lasting effect on how successful you will live the rest of your life as a born again believer. These spiritual disciplines, healthy relationships, and consistent fellowship with God's Word will strengthen your foundation and deepen your walk with Him.

The following basic steps will help reinforce your decision for Jesus Christ. However, if you ignore or discard the importance of this next moment it will reinforce the life you so desperately desire to escape. Let us help you, lead you, guide you, and walk with you through this journey, so that you will experience the love, joy, and peace of life in Christ. You were never meant to walk this path alone, and together we will grow, learn, and pursue everything God has prepared for you.

Again WELCOME TO THE FAMILY!

THE CHURCH

WHAT IS IT?

VERY FEW PEOPLE ACTUALLY UNDERSTAND the purpose of the church and why it is essential that they connect and attend consistently. Today, many people only think of the church as a building, but this is far from the biblical understanding. The word "church" comes from the Greek word "ecclesia" which is defined as "an assembly" or "called-out ones." So, the original meaning of "church" is not a building, but an assembly of people who have put their faith in Jesus Christ as Lord and Savior. 1 Peter 2:10 NIV Once you were not a people, but now you are the people of God; once you had not received mercy, but now you have received mercy.

The church is the Body of Christ, of which He

(Christ) is the head. Ephesians 1:22-23 says, "And God placed all things under his feet and appointed him to be head over everything for the church, which is his body, the fullness of him who fills everything in every way."

The Body of Christ is made up of all those who are true believers in Jesus Christ as the Son of God, and have accepted Him as their Lord and Savior. This assembly of believers has no racial, ethnical, religious, or economic distinctions. All those who have a personal relationship with Jesus Christ are part of the Body of Christ, and each believer should seek fellowship and edification in a local church. Within this community, believers discover their spiritual gifts and learn how to serve one another in love.

The local church is described in Galatians 1:1-2: "Paul, an apostle … and all the brothers with me, to the churches in Galatia." Here we see that in the province of Galatia there were many churches—what we call local churches. The local church is the place where the members of the Body of Christ receive encouragement, teaching, and accountability. These things are essential for new believers and older believers alike, to grow in the knowledge and grace of the Lord Jesus Christ.

> Ephesians 4:11 NIV "So Christ himself gave the apostles, the prophets, the evangelists, the pastors and teachers, 12 to equip his people for works of service, so that the body of Christ may be built up 13 until we all reach unity in the faith and in the knowledge of the Son of God and become mature, attaining to the whole measure of the fullness of Christ."

Again, this assembly is absolutely essential to the growth of each and every member of the Body of Christ and should not be forsaken or taken for granted.

Hebrews 10:25 NIV "Let us not give up meeting together, as some are in the habit of doing, but let us encourage one another—and all the more as you see the Day approaching."

In summary, the church is not a building or a denomination. According to the Bible, the church is the body of Christ—all those who have placed their faith in Jesus Christ for salvation. Local churches are gatherings of members of the Body of Christ.

Please Note:

Where you attend church is ABSOLUTELY ESSENTIAL. You need a biblically sound church! God did not leave this decision up to you. He said, "He would give you shepherds or pastors after His heart." Meaning He will give you the pastor best suited for you, even if you do not think so. Trust that God knows best.

Jeremiah 3:15 NKJV "And I will give you shepherds according to My heart, who will feed you with knowledge and understanding."

Additional Scripture Reading:

1 Corinthians 12:12 NIV Just as a body, though one, has many parts, but all its many parts form one body, so it is with Christ. 13 For we were all baptized by one Spirit so as to form one body—whether Jews or Gentiles, slave or free—and we were all given the one Spirit to drink. 14 Even so the body is not made up of one part but of many. 15 Now if the foot should say, "Because I am not a hand, I do not belong to the body," it would not for that reason stop being part of the body. 16 And if the ear should say, "Because I am not an eye, I do not belong to the body," it would not for that reason stop being part of the body. If the whole body were an eye, where would the sense of hearing be? 17 If the whole body were an ear, where would the sense of smell be? 18 But in fact God has placed the parts in the body, every one of them, just as he wanted them to be. 19 If they were all one part, where would the body be? 20 As it is, there are many

parts, but one body. 21 The eye cannot say to the hand, "I don't need you!" And the head cannot say to the feet, "I don't need you!" 22 On the contrary, those parts of the body that seem to be weaker are indispensable, 23 and the parts that we think are less honorable we treat with special honor. And the parts that are unpresentable are treated with special modesty, 24 while our presentable parts need no special treatment. But God has put the body together, giving greater honor to the parts that lacked it, 25 so that there should be no division in the body, but that its parts should have equal concern for each other. 26 If one part suffers, every part suffers with it; if one part is honored, every part rejoices with it. 27 Now you are the body of Christ, and each one of you is a part of it."

THE BIBLE

WHERE DO I START?

THE BIBLE IS THE MOST IMPORTANT BOOK IN the life of a Christian. Through the Bible we understand who God is, and more importantly, who we are as new believers in Jesus Christ. It helps us understand all that God has done for us and all that we can now do through Him. The Bible is way more than a simple book of do nots. It is way more than a book of rules. To the believer in Jesus Christ, it is our life and should never be discarded, nor should its importance be taken for granted!

2 Timothy 3:16 NIV "All Scripture is God-breathed and is useful for teaching, rebuking, correcting and training in righteousness, **17** so that the servant of God may be thoroughly equipped for every good work."

The Bible contains 66 books, divided into the Old and New Testaments with 1,189 chapters. As a new Christian, you must be asking, "Where do I start?" That is a great question! You can be sure that you will get different answers depending on who you ask. Some might say start in the beginning. Others may say start in the New Testament. The truth is, there is no right or wrong answer, only suggestions.

One thing you need to know is that the Bible is not like a novel or some kind of story book which reads smoothly from cover to cover. It is more like an all in one library or a collection of books written by many different authors who were led by the Spirit of God. As a new believer the best place to start is by reading the Gospels *(Matthew, Mark, Luke, and John)* as this will familiarize you with the person of Jesus, His life and His purpose.

Secondly, I suggest you read the books of *Romans*

and Ephesians both of which can be seen as the ABCs of Christianity. Reading these books should give you a really good start in becoming a well-informed Bible student. One last thing, remember this is not a sprint, this is a marathon. You do not have to read through the whole Bible in one day or in one setting. If you do, great. However, if you don't, do not feel bad. What you want to do is establish a daily practice of reading the word of God and spending time with God.

Additional Scripture Reading:

Psalms 119:105 NKJV "Your word is a lamp to my feet And a light to my path."

Isaiah 40:8 NKJV "The grass withers, the flower fades, But the word of our God stands forever."

Matthew 24:35 NKJV "Heaven and earth will pass away, but My words will by no means pass away."

John 8:31 NKJV "Then Jesus said to those Jews who believed Him, "If you abide in My word, you are My disciples indeed. **32** And you shall know the truth, and the truth shall make you free."

John 17:17 NKJV "Sanctify them by Your truth. Your word is truth."

James 1:22 NKJV "But be doers of the word, and not hearers only, deceiving yourselves."

PRAYER

WHAT DO I SAY?

THE ENGLISH DICTIONARY DEFINES PRAYER as "a solemn request for help" and this seems to be the basic understanding that people have about prayer. However, prayer is so much more than an emergency help line. It is so much more than an earnest hope or wish. If this is how prayer is viewed, then we will undoubtedly miss out on all of the benefits and beauty of this time spent with God the Father.

Prayer is simply, you as a newly born child of God and new follower of Jesus Christ communicating with your heavenly Father. He loves you and knows your every need, desire and concern and He wants you to communicate with him through prayer. One of the first requests of Jesus's disciples was "Lord teach us to pray."

> **Luke 11:1 NIV** "One day Jesus was praying in a certain place. When he finished, one of his disciples said to him, "Lord, teach us to pray, just as John taught his disciples.""

This tells us that knowing how to pray is not automatic and that there is a God designed way of effectively praying.

> **Matthew 6:9 NKJV** "In this manner, therefore, pray: Our Father in heaven, Hallowed be Your name. **10** Your kingdom come. Your will be done On earth as it is in heaven. **11** Give us this day our daily bread. **12** And forgive us our debts, As we forgive our debtors. **13** And do not lead us into temptation, But deliver us from the evil one. For Yours is the kingdom and the power and the glory forever. Amen."

This is known as the Lord's Prayer. Some people believe we should pray this exact prayer. However, Jesus did not mean for us to pray these specific words or in a particular manner. No, Jesus is simply giving us an example or road map to follow in our own personal time of prayer. However, all effective prayer has to have two elements. Regardless of what anyone might tell you, these two elements must be present if you desire to get the most out of your prayer time.

The first element is the Word of God. This is another reason why the Bible is important because our prayers cannot solely be based on our feelings, anxieties, or distresses. They cannot be based on what others think or suggest. Our prayers must be based on and founded in the Word of God.

1 John 5:14 NIV "This is the confidence we have in approaching God: that if we ask anything according to his will, he hears us. **15** And if we know that he hears us—whatever we ask—we know that we have what we asked of him."

The second essential element is faith because everything that God has done is only received by faith. Ok, I hear another question, "What is faith?" Faith is simply trust and dependency on God and in His Word.

James 1:5 NIV "If any of you lacks wisdom, you should ask God, who gives generously to all without finding fault, and it will be given to you. **6** But when you ask, you must believe and not doubt, because the one who doubts is like a wave of the sea, blown and tossed by the wind. **7** That person should not expect to receive anything from the Lord."

Developing the practice of daily communication with God through prayer cannot be overestimated. Why? Because through prayer we are strengthened. It is through prayer that we confess our sin and receive forgiveness. It is through prayer that we receive direction and learn the purpose of God for our lives. As we develop the practice of approaching God in prayer, we will come to know Him and draw ever nearer to Him. Our desires will become more like His.

> **1 Thessalonians 5:16 NIV** Rejoice always, **17** pray continually, **18** give thanks in all circumstances; for this is God's will for you in Christ Jesus."

In summary, prayer is not an emergency hot line system, nor is God simply someone you voice all of your complaints to. Prayer is your God given, God designed vehicle for communicating with Him. Finally, prayer is something that every Christian should do on a daily basis.

Additional Scripture Reading:

II Chronicles 7:14 NKJV "If My people who are called by My name will humble themselves, and pray and seek My face, and turn from their wicked ways, then I will hear from heaven, and will forgive their sin and heal their land. **15** Now My eyes will be open and My ears attentive to prayer made in this place."

Psalms 145:18 NKJV "The LORD is near to all who call upon Him, To all who call upon Him in truth."

Proverbs 3:5 NKJV "Trust in the LORD with all your heart, And lean not on your own understanding; **6** In all your ways acknowledge Him, And He shall direct your paths. **7** Do not be wise in your own eyes; Fear the LORD and depart from evil."

Philippians 4:6 NKJV "Be anxious for nothing, but

in everything by prayer and supplication, with thanksgiving, let your requests be made known to God; 7 and the peace of God, which surpasses all understanding, will guard your hearts and minds through Christ Jesus."

Colossians 4:2 NIV "Devote yourselves to prayer, being watchful and thankful."

ACTION STEPS

Step 1: THE CHURCH

Every born-again believer, absolutely without exception, needs to be connected to a Bible believing and teaching Church in order to get the most out of your new life in Christ. BE FAITHFUL, and commit to weekly attendance. Lastly, find a place to serve in the church, as faithfulness and serving are essential to your personal growth.

Step 2: THE BIBLE

This cannot be overstated. You must establish the practice of daily Bible reading. Just like your natural body needs food and water to live. Your spirit man needs the Word of God to live. Make an investment in your spiritual life by purchasing a good study bible.

Step 3: PRAYER

Daily communication with your Heavenly Father is essential. Again, He loves you and knows your every need, desire, and concern. He wants you to communicate with Him daily through prayer.

Again WELCOME TO THE FAMILY!